A KING IN HAITI

by Basil Heatter

THE BLACK COAST: The Story of the PT Boat

THE SEA DREAMERS

EIGHTY DAYS TO HONG KONG: The Story of the Clipper Ship

"WRECK ASHORE!"

AGAINST ODDS

A KING IN HAITI: The Story of Henri Christophe

The Story of Henri Christophe
A KING IN HAITI

by BASIL HEATTER

Illustrated by Toni Evins

FARRAR, STRAUS & GIROUX · NEW YORK

Text copyright © 1972 by Basil Heatter
Illustrations copyright © 1972 by Farrar, Straus & Giroux, Inc.
All rights reserved
First printing, 1972
Library of Congress catalog card number 72–184125
ISBN 0-374-34140-0
Printed in the United States of America
Published simultaneously in Canada by Doubleday Canada Ltd., Toronto
Designed by Bobye List

1698041

TO MAIDA AND RALPH
WITH GRATITUDE AND AFFECTION

Author's Note

During the time of Henri Christophe, Haiti was in a highly confused state. Political control shifted frequently and rapidly, and even seemingly authoritative accounts of the period are not always in complete agreement as to the course of events. Rather than attempt to present the full and detailed political and military picture, which could be of only slight interest to the average young reader, in this book I have tried to focus on Christophe himself and on the events that shaped his life.

All the facts concerning Christophe's life are not known, and even some of those most generally held cannot be completely substantiated. In telling Christophe's story, I have drawn on the facts available, using storyteller's license only to supply probable details.

B.H.

PROLOGUE

The island bulges from the sea like a great green frog. Its humped back is spiny-ridged. Its name, Haiti, comes from the Indian meaning "high place." Long ago—when the events told in this book were taking place—it was known as Saint Domingue. It is a strange, ghostly place with a history so blood-soaked as to make it unique in our hemisphere.

On the northern coast of Haiti, brooding over the sea at an altitude of 2,600 feet, sits an immense ruin, once a mighty fortress and still one of the world's wonders. This wedge-shaped structure can be seen twenty miles at sea, and on a moonlit night when clouds race overhead, it seems to push through the sky like a full-rigged ship. Bats are the only inhabitants now of its dark caverns. All around stand rusty guns like a circle of silent sentinels. It is said that twenty thousand men died building this immense structure and their bones still lie in the thick jungle below. But the bones of the king who conceived this mighty undertaking and ordered it built lie within. His name was Henri I.

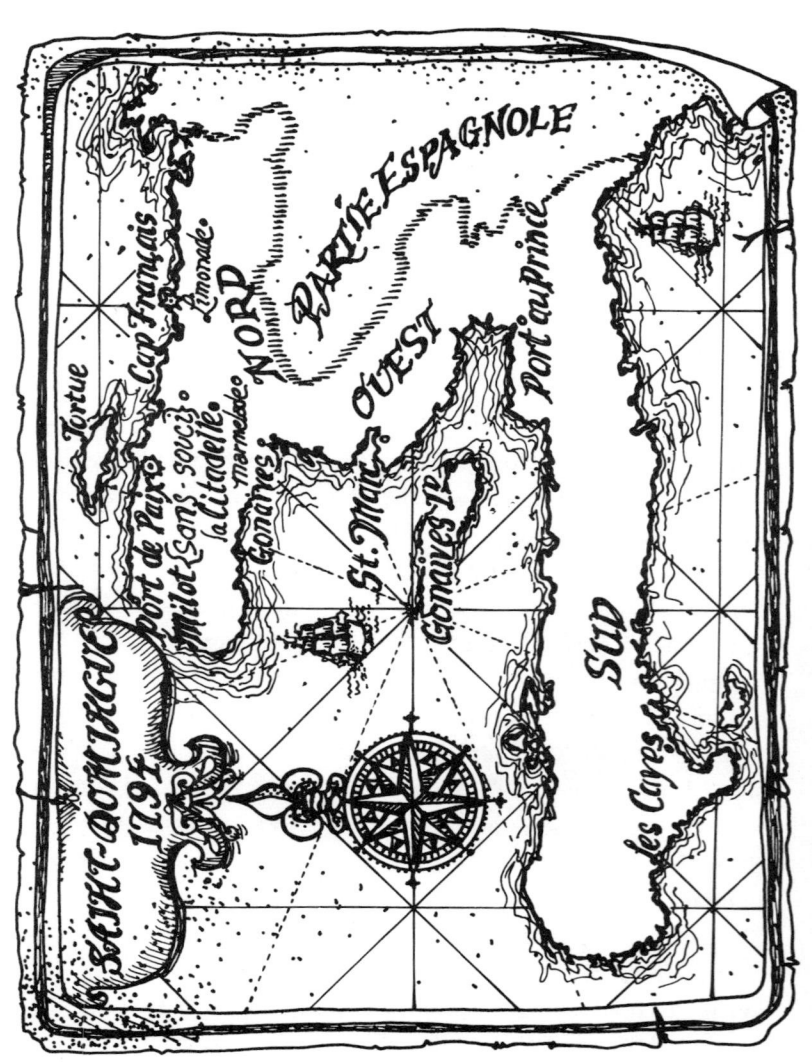

1

NO ONE KNEW where he came from. Some said the island of Saint Kitts and others Grenada. Only one thing about Henri Christophe's history is certain: his father was a slave. Like all the other slave children who grew up on the islands of the West Indies, Christophe never learned to read or write. There were no schools for slave children, and until they were old enough for heavy labor, their time was spent running through the green forests and bathing in the mountain streams.

Even as a child, Christophe seemed set apart from the others. He was taller and stronger and carried himself with a kind of natural dignity that seemed out of place for the son of a slave. No one could have known then that it was the dignity of a king.

The drowsy days of childhood drifted by, the only really carefree days he would ever know. Rainclouds rolled down from the mountains, bringing moisture for the soil. The great fields of sugar cane flourished under the hot sun. The slaves rose at dawn and went out into the fields with their cutting knives. When the cane had been cut, it was assembled in bundles and carried to the mills. Slave children sometimes went with their mothers to the fields, sometimes wandered off to play or to swim in one of the mountain streams. Henri probably played the games that children have always played—games of war with sticks for muskets. Perhaps he was the general—General Henri Christophe, barefoot, dusty and laughing in the sun.

In 1774, when he was seven, Henri's carefree childhood ended. He was sold to a stonemason who put him to work carrying bricks and mortar. From dawn to dusk he labored in the heat, and when night fell, he was glad of his straw pallet. Though the work was hard, it was not unrewarding, for he was learning much about the art of masonry, lessons that were put to good use when the time came to build the great fortress on the mountain.

What he learned too in those years was the simple lesson that, though he was black and a slave, he was still a man, not a beast of burden. By the time he was twelve, he was almost full grown, and he knew that, come what may, he would not spend the rest of his life trudging from one brick pile to another in return for scraps of food and a place to lay his head.

On his twelfth birthday he ran away, hiding in the hold of a French ship moored in the harbor. He was not discovered until the ship was well out to sea. Dragged up to face the captain, Henri held himself erect, not cowering in fear, as might have been expected. The Frenchman saw no point in mistreating the boy. He was tall and strong and would fetch a good price at the nearest market.

As it turned out, the first slave market they would come to was at Saint Domingue. Until then, Henri was put to work as a sailor. As the ship sailed north, the islands fell away like a row of stepping stones, and at last the brooding peaks of the French colony of Saint Domingue rose above the horizon. Henri knew that he would be sold back into slavery as soon as he was ashore, but even as a slave his prospects at Saint Domingue, richest island in the Caribbean, would be better than elsewhere. Cap Français, the principal city on the north coast, was a town of broad avenues, parks and fine homes unlike any Henri had ever seen before. A squadron of French naval vessels lay in the harbor, flags snapping in the breeze. Carriages drawn by beautiful horses deposited passengers at the wharf. Uniformed officers sat drinking, in the shade of striped awnings. Wealthy planters in broad-

brimmed straw hats bargained for goods in the warehouses. He was aware of a constant air of bustle and commerce such as he had never known on the sleepy little island from which he had escaped.

Even for a slave there had to be an opportunity in such a place, perhaps even to the point where he might some day buy his freedom. Unafraid, Henri stepped forward to be sold.

It was a bit of luck for the boy that he was not sold straight into the backbreaking labor of the cane fields. Instead, he was bought by a naval officer who wanted a boy to shine his boots and wait on him in the mess. And almost at once Henri found himself at sea again, this time heading north to help the struggling young republic that called itself the United States.

There were twenty-four ships of the line under the command of a French admiral, a magnificent sight in that year of 1779. Their mission had come about as a result of the visit to Paris of the American ambassador, Benjamin Franklin. When Franklin had presented his credentials to the king of France, he had been so eloquent in pleading the cause of the revolutionists that the king was persuaded to order his naval squadron north to Savannah.

The French ships reached the mouth of the Savannah River on the coast of Georgia and spent a month there at anchor in squally weather. Their presence may have bolstered the hopes of the young republic, but the French squadron did not participate actively in the military campaign against the British. All the same, it was Christophe's first exposure to the ideals of liberty and equality and no doubt a revelation to him to find thousands of men—black and white—risking their lives for the cause of freedom.

2

TWO MONTHS LATER the fleet returned to Saint Domingue and Henri was sold again, this time to a free Negro who owned a small hotel on the waterfront. He became a stableboy, cleaning and feeding the horses of guests who dismounted in the courtyard. He was not mistreated and in time his Negro master came to think of him almost as a son. Eventually he was promoted from the stable to the position of waiter in the dining room.

This was an enviable job, for he was able to save a little money—an almost unheard-of privilege for a slave. Rich planters befuddled with rum were apt to be free with their tips. Henri took the coins they gave him and hid them behind the stable. Hardly any of it was spent. He was saving that money toward the day when he would buy his freedom.

Social life in Saint Domingue was based entirely

on color and so it was almost incredibly complicated. There were 250 official varieties of racial strain, each with its own niche. The white Frenchman was at the top of the social ladder and the black at the bottom, but in between were the mulattoes, those of mixed blood. The population consisted of 40,000 whites, 24,000 mulattoes and almost half a million black slaves. The result was a mixture of furious jealousies and class hatreds.

Although the mulattoes were free, they were never on an equal social basis with the whites. Mulatto soldiers wore different uniforms than the whites, and even the wealthiest mulatto planters, whose children were educated in the best universities in Paris, were forbidden by law to wear clothing which might be considered competitive with that worn by the whites.

The formula for discrimination was simple. Since the white was at the top of the pyramid and the black at the bottom, it must follow that the half-white was in between and the quarter-white a step below, and so on down through every possible variation.

It was a volcanic situation and the explosion was not long in coming.

The first hint of trouble came from overseas. The Bastille had fallen in 1789 and the French Revolution was a fact. The words Freedom, Liberty and Equality were now being used in Cap Français. Saint Domingue, locked for so many years in brooding silence, was beginning to stir.

Christophe, still a waiter, was then in his early twenties—a tall, straight-featured, broad-shouldered man who gave the impression of biding his time. He did not join in the heated arguments over racial equality but listened carefully, trying to sift fact from rumor. The air was alive with stories, many of which were true. A white man had been dragged from his house and had been beheaded by a mob of other whites for daring to suggest reforms which would have favored the mulattoes. Another had been tied to the tail of a horse and pulled through the streets. Mobs of whites were attacking the sugar refineries of rich mulattoes. Two mulatto agitators had been tortured to death on the rack while the crowds along the waterfront sipped their drinks and watched the show.

The fuse had been lit. Although the French Revolution had taken place three thousand miles away, it was to become the single most important event in the history of the West Indies. Christophe heard it argued all around him. And he was aware that it was being discussed in other places as well—around smoky fires in hidden places in the jungle, where slaves were violating the law which forbade them to meet in secret. The word revolution had been sounded on the drums and was being carried by the wind. Many whites were beginning to leave Saint Domingue. The others waited for the first blow.

The revolutionaries met secretly by night in a dense part of the forest called the Alligator Wood. Most of the talk was hearsay, but the rumors were in themselves explosive. It had been reported that the new republican government in Paris had forbidden planters to whip their slaves. Since the planters were disobeying the order, an army would be sent from France to punish them. There was no truth to either story, but they were sparks rising from a smoldering fire.

These meetings in the forest were a curious combination of political agitation and savage celebration. The drums carried word of the time and place. Silently the shadowy figures emerged from the forest into the glow of torches stuck in the ground. There was talk of revolution and bloody murder and death.

Most of the men who came were giants, their bodies hardened by years of heavy work and sparse diet. But among them was a small, wizened coachman who drove a carriage for hire around the docks of Cap Français. Although he was physically no match for the others, he had a remarkable mind. His name was Toussaint and eventually he would come

to be known as Toussaint Louverture. Toussaint the Opener. It was Toussaint who would open a new way of life for them all, but at the moment he did not believe they were ready for open rebellion. He advocated caution and watchfulness while the whites and mulattoes attacked each other. He was shouted down.

Eight days after the last of several meetings in the Alligator Wood—on the night of August 22, 1791—the smoldering rebellion flared into open revolt. That night the tom-toms, sounding from valley to valley and from peak to peak, took on a note of frenzy. The whites were awakened in their beds by the ferocious drumming. The slaves gripped their machetes and rose from their mats. Torches flared against the velvet blackness of the forest. A great spurt of flame marked a burning plantation house. Then another. And another. By morning more than a hundred fires were raging and five hundred planters and their families had been murdered.

The dance of death went on night and day for a week, and at the end of it six hundred plantations and two hundred sugar refineries had been destroyed. Among the blacks who took no part in the bloodletting were Toussaint and Christophe. They argued for restraint, not out of pity for the whites but because they felt it was too soon. The blacks were untrained, they warned; the real leaders had not yet taken command. The black rabble would be defeated by the well-armed white and mulatto soldiers. Again they were shouted down.

At the end of a week, it was over. The slaves attempted a frontal attack on Cap Français and were quickly scattered by the well-organized defenders. Nothing was left to mark the revolt but the ashes of the burned plantations, the grief of the bereaved and the grinning heads of the black leaders mounted on stakes at the entrance to the city.

3

IN 1793—two years after the first revolt—the moment for which Toussaint had been waiting was at hand. France was at war with Spain and England and could do little to aid the whites on Saint Domingue. Toussaint organized an army of runaway slaves and led them across to the Spanish side of the island. The black army was greeted warmly there and Toussaint was appointed their commanding general.

Thus, Saint Domingue was torn apart by conflicting armies. The blacks, under Toussaint, held most of the north and east of the country, while an invading English force from Jamaica occupied Port-au-Prince, a major city in the south. Toussaint had command of four thousand well-trained troops, but he felt no strong sense of loyalty to Spain. He had been forced by events to fight against his own country but his emotional ties were still with Saint Domingue and even with France.

In August of 1793 he addressed a message to all the blacks on the island:

> Brothers and Friends:
> I am Toussaint Louverture; my name is perhaps known to you. I have undertaken to avenge your wrongs. It is my desire that liberty and equality shall reign in Saint Domingue. I am striving to this end. Come and unite with us, brothers, and fight for the same cause.

Almost on the heels of that message Toussaint did an about-face and joined forces with the French general defending Port-de-Paix. It was a move that has since been criticized as traitorous, but it must be viewed in the light of Toussaint's real allegiance, which was not to the Spaniards or to the French but to his fellow blacks.

In any case, his defection brought about a reversal of the balance of power. Within a few weeks the Spaniards had given up every position they had been holding and Toussaint was in high favor with the French.

The little coachman was now the major figure in Haitian life, but he was under no delusion that the peace which had settled on the island was anything but temporary. True, the slaves had been freed by a

decree issued in Paris in February 1794, but there was no guarantee that the policies of the white planters might not again prevail in Paris and that the French might not send another army to return Toussaint and his people to slavery. He was determined to build a black army which would be strong enough to prevent that, and in his search for good men he began a serious recruiting campaign.

Among those who answered the call was Henri Christophe. Christophe was by then twenty-seven, a gigantic figure of a man who attracted attention wherever he went. Little is known of his early years in the army except that his rise was astonishingly rapid. Within seven years he had gone from sergeant to general with rank second only to that of

Toussaint himself. It was a rise almost as rapid as that of the great Napoleon Bonaparte, at that moment the most powerful figure in Europe. Who could have foreseen that these two men—the black former slave and the white former corporal—would one day oppose each other in battle?

Christophe had come as far in his own small world as Napoleon had in his much larger one. The onetime slave was now the commanding general in Cap Français and owned the finest home on Saint Domingue. Rugs and draperies had been imported from Paris, marble floors from Italy, paneling from Honduras. And Christophe dressed in a manner that matched his style of living. He designed his own uniforms, with great gold epaulets and cocked hats. Flamboyant as the uniforms were, they seemed a perfect match for his immense frame. In appearance he might have been a king or an emperor.

Christophe still had not learned to read or write, but that was not unusual for a Haitian general. The qualities that were required were courage, tenacity, physical strength and natural intelligence, and these he had in abundance. When the time came, he would learn to write his name and one more word: *Roi*—King.

Peace had come to Europe, and Napoleon now found himself the world's most powerful ruler. It was time to turn his attention to the lost colony of Saint Domingue. Considerable pressure was being brought to bear on him to subdue the former slaves and return the island to white rule. Who was this ugly little coachman Toussaint who now had the temerity to set himself up as governor general of what had once been France's richest colony? Who was this hulking waiter Christophe who dressed like a field marshal and lived in a palace? Almost every day the influential planters who had fled to Paris brought additional pressure to bear. The wealth which had accumulated from Saint Domingue's sun-drenched plains and fertile soil—the seemingly endless supply of coffee and sugar—could not be abandoned to the blacks. At first Bonaparte discouraged such talk, but in time he came to listen to it.

Napoleon was unquestionably the greatest military genius of his time, and his plan for the reconquest of Saint Domingue was on a par with the rest of his campaigns. Not that he believed that so much force would be necessary to overwhelm the black rabble, but that in this case force would be an adjunct to diplomacy. When the blacks saw the size of the army he would send, they would surrender in short order.

Slowly the project took shape in his mind. To begin with, his troops would have to be transported, and for this he would need a fleet—the largest invasion fleet Europe had seen since the Spanish Armada. Twenty-two thousand men were to be taken overseas, and this was no small undertaking, even for Bonaparte. Six of France's largest shipyards were put to work on the project. Eighty-six ships would be required. It would take time and money, but now that France was at peace for the first time in so many years, Bonaparte had plenty of both.

His armies were undefeated, having achieved all he had sought in Europe, but it would not do to leave them idle too long. Fighting men could not be kept at the peak of efficiency in peacetime. This little venture to Saint Domingue would be a splendid way to keep them busy. And at the same time, it would help solve another problem. Bonaparte's younger sister, Pauline, had married one of his most dashing generals, Charles Leclerc. Leclerc's rise had been almost as meteoric as that of Bonaparte. He had enlisted as an ordinary soldier, risen to captain and then had been appointed general during the campaign in Italy. It was indicative of Napoleon's confidence in his young general that he had done all in his power to bring about the marriage of Pauline and Leclerc.

But Leclerc was restless in Paris. He was a straightforward soldier and war was his natural element. This Haitian campaign might be the perfect thing for him. And it would be amusing for Pauline, as the wife of the governor general, to dominate the social life of the island. She could establish her court in Cap Français—at that time the principal city—and give the sort of lavish parties for which she had become famous. The adventure was appealing from every standpoint.

Still, Napoleon did not underestimate the blacks; he was far too canny a general for that. He would send five times the force that was actually required, he would use every sort of trickery to separate the black leaders from their followers.

With this in mind, he prepared careful instructions for Leclerc, outlining the way in which Toussaint and the other black generals would first be treated as equals and even allies and then, as quickly and unobtrusively as possible, be put on board ship and sent to France, where they would either be imprisoned or exiled. As part of this plan, Bonaparte even went so far as to curry favor with Toussaint's two sons, who were at school in Paris. It was arranged that they should travel back to Saint Domingue with Leclerc's force in order to reassure their father of Bonaparte's peaceful intentions and persuade him to return to Paris with the ships.

Thus, the adventure took shape. The huge fleet was assembled and the army put on board. Leclerc and Pauline supervised the loading of their household goods. Flags whipped in the breeze and cannon on the shore sounded a salute as the ships raised anchor. Sails were got up and one after another the ships headed westward toward the open Atlantic. Bonaparte was convinced that in this case, as with everything else he had accomplished in life, careful preparation would be the key to victory. The way had been thoroughly prepared for this mighty fleet he was sending to Saint Domingue.

The mountains of Haiti rose above the horizon on the morning of February 3, 1802, as the great fleet came to anchor in the roadstead off Cap Français. Leclerc was not anticipating any problem in making a landing, but he was not taking any chances. He had not brought his entire force to Cap Français. Three divisions under different generals were also approaching the island at other points, to create diversionary attacks if necessary. Leclerc's reservations, if any, had only to do with the size of his force. Surely one division of the best troops in Europe would have been enough to conquer these savages. In his own mind he was quite sure that Bonaparte had overestimated Toussaint's strength.

It was beneath Leclerc's dignity to come ashore personally to meet with Christophe, the commanding general at Cap Français. Instead, he sent a young officer named LeBrun to tell Christophe to prepare the town for the formal debarkation of Leclerc and his army.

The small boat pulled away from the ship with LeBrun sitting in the stern. The boat was rowed across the harbor and brought to a landing at the main wharf. Christophe was there waiting.

LeBrun offered a formal salute, which was scrupulously returned. This first meeting left an indelible impression on the young Frenchman. He had never before seen such a giant of a man or one so elaborately uniformed. Christophe welcomed LeBrun with grave courtesy and led him to a beautifully varnished carriage drawn by two white horses. Together they rode through the streets of Cap Français to the governor's palace.

If LeBrun had expected native huts and shabby peasants, he was in for a rude surprise. They traveled along broad avenues lined with fine homes. Nor did the Frenchman fail to note the black soldiers stationed in front of every public building, each one carrying an unlit torch.

LeBrun, acting as Leclerc's messenger, carried with him letters to Toussaint. When told that Toussaint was not at Cap Français but in the south, he refused to turn the letters over to Christophe. He did, however, intimate that if Christophe were to surrender the city before Toussaint's arrival Leclerc would be favorably impressed and would undoubtedly reward Christophe in suitable fashion.

Christophe listened in silence. They were at dinner in the immense paneled dining room, eating from Christophe's gold plates. Around them sat Christophe's aides. When the Frenchman had finished, Christophe rose and, drawing himself to his full height, asked, in a voice which rang through the hall, if LeBrun was suggesting that he engage in treason against Toussaint. Despite the great army which lay at anchor in the harbor, LeBrun was for the moment at Christophe's mercy. Christophe could have broken him with one hand. LeBrun hastened to assure him that what he was suggesting was not treason but rather submission to an overpowering force.

"Do you think," asked Christophe, "that you have but to show your ships and men to get me to betray my trust to Governor Toussaint and the people of Saint Domingue? I am a soldier and I will obey my orders, but I will obey no orders other than those of Governor Toussaint. You may rest here tonight and no one will harm you, but tomorrow you will be returned to your ships, and I would advise you to keep them well clear of my cannon until the arrival of Governor Toussaint."

Next morning LeBrun was escorted back to the

wharf. This time Christophe did not go with him. The boat was waiting and LeBrun was rowed across to the flagship. The story he had to tell was hardly what Leclerc had been waiting to hear. These were no simple natives who could be overcome by guile or half promises. Christophe wore the uniform of a full general of France and carried himself accordingly. They had dined off golden plates in a palace and LeBrun had observed at least fifty cannon ringing the harbor. In addition, Christophe had made it clear that if the French attempted a landing by force before Toussaint's arrival, the city would be put to the torch and totally destroyed.

Angrily, Leclerc dashed off a note to Christophe:

> I learn with indignation, Citizen General, that you refuse to receive the squadron of the French army which I command, under the pretext that you have no order from the Governor General. I avow it will distress me to have to count you among the rebels. I warn you that if today you have not delivered all the batteries of the coast, tomorrow at daybreak, 15,000 men will be disembarked . . . I hold you responsible.
>
> LECLERC

Christophe's dictated reply came back by the same boat:

> I have dispatched one of my aides to Governor Toussaint Louverture to inform him of your arrival. Until his re-

ply reaches me, I cannot permit you to disembark. If you have the force with which you threaten me, I shall offer you all the resistance which marks a general. If the chance of war favors you, you will enter the city of the Cap only when it has been reduced to ashes, and even on the ashes I will still fight you. As to the troops that you say you will disembark, I look upon them as so many cards that the least wind will blow down . . .

As to the loss of your esteem, General, I assure you I do not want it at the price you put upon it, if it must cause me to act contrary to my duty.

H. CHRISTOPHE

But Leclerc was not to be put off with an exchange of letters. Bonaparte's opening gambit, an attempt to seduce Christophe away from Toussaint and thus divide the resistance, had failed. It was time now to forget such timid diplomacy and resort to power. Forty-eight hours went by with no further exchange between the generals. At the end of that time, Leclerc made his landing. But no sooner had the first Frenchman set foot on shore than pillars of smoke began rising from the city. Christophe was being as good as his word: he was putting the city to the torch. Leclerc had the strength to take the city, but when he did, he would find only ashes.

Christophe's own mansion had been the first to go. He had put the flame to it with his own hand, an action taken despite the objections of all the leading

citizens of the city and most of his own officers. It had resulted in an immediate loss of loyalty. Most of Christophe's army, feeling that the city was being destroyed in a useless gesture, had deserted overnight and he was left now with only a few hundred men. He was no longer in a position to offer any organized resistance.

The fire raged throughout the city. Out of eight hundred major buildings, only sixty remained. Pauline Bonaparte's dream of a gay, carefree round of parties in the sunny city of the Cap had gone up in smoke. So too had Leclerc's notion of a triumphal entry. The great Bonaparte's strategy had failed.

From a hilltop beyond the city, Christophe watched the French make their landing. With a grin, he swept off his elaborate hat and made them a low bow. Then he mounted his white horse and set off into the hills to find Toussaint.

4

CHRISTOPHE HAD MADE a dramatic and ruinously expensive gesture in the hope that it would unite his people in resistance to the invaders. He was to be disappointed. To Christophe, this resistance was a necessary part of the original revolt against white oppression. He was convinced that the blacks would never be allowed to live as free equals once the white planters regained control and that Napoleon's promises to the contrary were so many scraps of paper. The French had come, talking peace but with an army of twenty thousand men at their backs. They were prepared for war and war was what he would give them.

What he failed to take into account was the lack of support among his own people. They were sick of war. Bonaparte had promised that slavery was finished and they believed him. What they wanted now was not more killing but time to cultivate their land and produce their crops. If Toussaint and Christophe wanted war, that was their business; they would have to go it alone.

There were three small forces offering resistance to the invaders—one under Toussaint, another under Christophe and the third under another black general and former slave named Dessalines. Although both Christophe and Dessalines had sworn loyalty to Toussaint, they had little love for each other and before the arrival of the French had been on the verge of war with each other.

Initially, it appeared that the cause of the black generals was hopeless. Outnumbered and outgunned and lacking the support of their own people, they could do little but fade away before the advancing French, destroying towns and plantations as they retreated. Throughout the campaign Leclerc never lost a battle; on the other hand, he could never quite win the war. His troops were growing weary of the apparently endless pursuit over rugged mountains and across scorching plains. Moreover, they could not help but feel a certain sympathy for the men they were chasing. They themselves had only recently thrown off the shackles of monarchy. *Liberté* had been the watchword of their own revolution, and they were beginning to wonder why they had been sent so far to fight against these former slaves who were ready to die for the same ideal.

But worst of all was the incessant heat and the tropical fevers. Leclerc, in a letter to Paris, tried to give some impression of the difficulties he was facing:

> It is absolutely necessary to see the country to form an adequate idea of the difficulties which it presents at every step. I have never seen in the Alps any obstacles equal to those with which it abounds.

The black generals were well aware that white men could not fight on indefinitely under such conditions. They hoped that in time the enemy would begin to sicken and die. At best it was a forlorn hope. By the end of February, three weeks after the landing at Cap Français, the French were in possession of all the principal towns. Toussaint and Christophe were still offering some small resistance, but they were regarded now as little more than common outlaws. It was at that moment that Dessalines, Christophe's rival, wrote to Toussaint to urge him to continue the resistance:

> Nothing is hopeless, Citizen General, if you can but deprive the invaders of the resources of Port-au-Prince. Try to burn that place by every means of force and guile. Watch for the moment when the garrison is weakened by

expeditions into the plains, and then try to surprise and capture the town behind them. Do not forget that while we are waiting for the rainy season, which should rid us of our enemies, our resources are destruction and fire. Ambush the roads; throw dead men and horses into the wells. Destroy all, burn all, so that those who come here to force us back into slavery may have ever before their eyes the image of that hell which they desire.

Dessalines's advice came too late. Toussaint, far from being in a position to burn Port-au-Prince, was in fact surrounded and close to defeat. He had managed to slip through the French lines into the Artibonite Valley but was trapped there in his last stronghold.

Leclerc was elated. So far as he could see, the war was over and he had accomplished everything that Bonaparte had expected. He had only to take Toussaint now, dead or alive, to end the campaign. Dessalines and Christophe were completely isolated, and once he had finished Toussaint, all resistance would be over. Satisfied that it would be the final battle, he ordered an assault on Toussaint's hilltop position. But what Leclerc had thought of as hardly more than a skirmish turned out to be the fiercest battle of the war. Wave after wave of French soldiers struggled toward the summit only to be turned back by the fanatical defenders. Before the day was over, fifteen hundred Frenchmen lay on the slopes and the position was still untaken. Furious at this bloody repulse, Leclerc ordered a nonstop bombardment. The artillery assault went on for three days and then the French stormed the summit, only to find Toussaint gone. The black leader and half a dozen of his men had cut their way through the French lines and escaped once more.

Leclerc took little joy in his victory. He had destroyed the black armies, but the cost had been atrociously high. In two months of fighting, he had lost seven thousand of his best troops, almost half his effective fighting force. The tiresome and ugly war was stretching into months.

Leclerc now undertook to remove Christophe once and for all from the fighting. Through a former friend of Christophe's, Leclerc arranged to have a letter delivered to the general in which he promised that under no circumstances would slavery ever again be tolerated on the island. In addition, he offered Christophe a full pardon and money enough to leave Saint Domingue and live wherever he chose.

The letter was delivered to Christophe at his camp in the hills. The general, dressed in rags, his belly growling with hunger, listened in brooding silence while the letter was read aloud. Sweat rolled down his face from beneath his ruined hat. He looked at his starving men and the useless muskets, long since empty of ammunition. He knew what was passing through their minds. The war was over. It had brought nothing but death and destruction. To fight on a few more days or weeks would accomplish nothing but the death of them all. For the moment at least, the French had won. It was time to go home.

5

THEY RODE DOWN out of the hills into Cap Français, a gigantic black man on a white horse trailed by no more than a dozen barefoot men. He had expected nothing but hatred from the citizens of the Cap. He had burned their city and had failed in his war with the French. Yet there was nothing apologetic about the way he held himself in the saddle, eyes locked straight ahead, cocked hat set at a jaunty angle.

To his surprise, he found that much of what he had destroyed had already been rebuilt. Even more surprising was the welcome he received. The streets were decorated with flags and flowers. They were welcoming the general home. True, he had lost a war, but he had fought against overwhelming odds until the end. More important, though, he was *their* general, a black man who had roared his defiance at Napoleon. It had been a magnificent gesture, one the

blacks would never forget. Now they came to do him honor. Even Toussaint, who surrendered a few days later, would not receive so extravagant a reception. Last of the rebellious generals to surrender was Dessalines. Of them all, he made his hatred for the whites most evident. Even while he, like Christophe, was being installed as a general in the French army, he kept his back to the French commanders. He had sworn never again to look a white man in the face, and he was as good as his word.

What of Toussaint? Unlike Christophe and Dessalines, who were in the prime of life, Toussaint was now old and broken. He wanted no more of fighting or of power. He had lived to see slavery abolished and his people free, and all he wanted now was to retire to his small farm near Gonaïves. When he made this wish known to Leclerc, the Frenchman accepted the idea with enthusiasm, even going so far as to suggest that Toussaint could make his retirement more interesting by preparing helpful hints on administration for the new government.

But, as it turned out, Leclerc had no intention of letting Toussaint live out his remaining years at Gonaïves. He arranged to have the old soldier invited to dinner at the home of a French general named Brunet. Toussaint might have scented a trap in these rather cumbersome arrangements, but he had no reason to suppose the French still regarded him as any sort of menace. Halfway through dinner, a dozen armed men burst into the room and seized Toussaint. With a saber at his throat, he was disarmed and hustled downstairs. Bound and gagged, he was thrown into a small boat and rowed across to a French frigate which was already making sail.

So much for Leclerc's promise of a peaceful retirement. Toussaint the "Opener," the father of modern-day Haiti, the liberator of his people, was being taken away to a French prison like a common criminal. Through anguished eyes the old man watched the green rim of his beloved island sink beneath the horizon. It was the last he would ever see of it.

Upon his arrival in France, Toussaint was imprisoned in a dungeon in the cold, bleak Jura Mountains. Accustomed as he was to the tropics, he was gripped by the cold of those stone walls as by an icy hand. He wrote letter after letter to Bonaparte, requesting the same kind of hearing that would have been given to any ordinary felon. But no hearing was granted. Toussaint was as cut off from the world as if he had been put into a tomb. He managed to survive one winter, but he could never make it through the second. Repeatedly, he asked for news of his wife and children, but no news was ever given to him. On

April 27, 1803, the old warrior's heart gave up the unequal struggle. Toussaint died in his cell. Napoleon had won his final battle with the old man.

Perhaps it might have been some satisfaction to Toussaint to know that Napoleon himself would one day die in exile, also a prisoner, and that Leclerc, too, young and vigorous as he was, would soon follow Toussaint to the grave.

For despite Leclerc's apparent victory and the removal of Toussaint, fear was spreading like the shadow of a giant hand across Saint Domingue. An unexpected ally had come to the aid of the blacks, an enemy before whom Leclerc with all his guns and ships was helpless. Out of the swamps and across the mist-shrouded hills spread an epidemic of yellow fever, a disease from which blacks were spared but which shriveled the whites where they stood.

As the epidemic took hold, an air of desperate gaiety gripped the whites in Cap Français. The parties became longer and more lavish than ever, but at virtually every one some young officer dropped in his tracks and his unconscious body was hustled outside while the others tried to carry on as though nothing had happened. Leclerc's magnificent army was melting away before his eyes. The fever spared no one, striking as quickly at generals as at privates.

As the plague spread, so did rebellion. Leclerc was finding that his war was not over after all. Farms were attacked again, French settlers murdered in their beds. Enraged, Leclerc struck back. He ordered Christophe and Dessalines to disarm the peasants. The two black generals acknowledged the orders and disappeared into the hills. They would carry out the order to the letter, but what they would do with the arms once they had got them was something an officer more imaginative than Leclerc might have foreseen.

6

TIME WAS RUNNING OUT for Leclerc. His European troops were dying at an appalling rate and his black troops were showing signs of revolt. His dispatches to Napoleon were becoming frantic cries for help:

> My position grows worse from day to day, and the most terrible thing about the situation is that I cannot tell you when or how it will improve. September has cost me more than four thousand dead. If the disease should continue with this intensity, the colony is lost.
> Each day the insurgent forces increase, while mine diminish by loss of whites and desertions of the blacks. Never was a general in a more dreadful situation. The troops that arrived a month ago no longer exist. Each day the rebels attack and firing can be heard in the Cap. I cannot take the offensive with the men I have, and even should I attack, I could not follow up the victories I might gain. I repeat what I have said before; Saint Domingue

is lost to France if by the end of January I do not receive ten thousand men in a body.

The following day he issued an even more frantic call:

> You will never subdue Saint Domingue without an army of twelve thousand acclimated troops, and you will not have this army until you have sent seventy thousand men.

It was to be the captain general's last call for help. He had finally come to the realization that Bonaparte either would not or could not send him reinforcements. Leclerc's position was desperate. Virtually all his colonial troops had deserted, and the hospitals were crowded with dying French soldiers. Leclerc had only two hundred men left in his garrison at the Cap. Perhaps at that moment he was remembering Christophe's answer when the great French fleet had appeared off the coast and Leclerc had threatened to put fifteen thousand men ashore.

> As to the troops that you say you will disembark, I look upon them as so many cards that the least wind will blow down...

So Christophe had written and so it had proved to be. On October 7, 1802, Leclerc wrote his last letter:

Here is my opinion of this country: We must destroy all the mountain Negroes, men and women, sparing only children under twelve years of age. We must destroy half the Negroes of the plains and not allow in the colony a single man who has worn an epaulet. Without these measures, the colony will never be at peace, and every year, especially deadly ones like this, you will have a civil war on your hands which will jeopardize the future.

Leclerc was already gripped by malaria when he wrote that letter. Lank, sweating, barely able to walk, he attempted to inspect his defenses but had not the strength. He was put to bed and shortly thereafter the first symptoms of yellow fever appeared. For eleven days the strong young captain general battled against approaching death, but on the twelfth he died, raving.

Pauline Bonaparte, who had come to Saint Domingue with visions of becoming a sort of New World empress, fled back to France on the same ship that carried her husband's body. The great adventure was over and the mighty Napoleon had suffered his first defeat. True, he had been defeated not so much by enemy guns as by the mosquitoes that carried the fever, but all the same, the taste of defeat was bitter.

Leclerc was replaced by his second in command, a former planter named Rochambeau, who now took over a skeleton army and a lost cause. He made no secret of his pathological hatred of the black population, even going so far as to import giant bloodhounds which were trained to attack any black on sight. Sunday afternoons were devoted to the training of these dogs and there was always a live black subject to be served up to them. On other occasions, blacks suspected of traitorous impulses were chained together in a long line and tossed from the deck of a ship into the harbor while Rochambeau nodded approvingly.

But oppression only bred increasing resistance. Christophe, who was somewhere in the hills with the thirty thousand rifles he had obligingly collected in the name of Leclerc, had returned to open rebellion. So too had the brutal Dessalines. Rochambeau responded by drowning two thousand blacks at a public massacre. Dessalines, the only one who could unite the blacks and mulattoes, took over the command of all rebel forces. Once more the fighting began, this time against the seriously weakened, almost decimated French forces. Rochambeau was forced to give up one position after another. Dessalines and Christophe moved inexorably down out of the hills, until at last the French held only Cap Français.

With their backs to the sea, the French fought bravely, but it was the last battle. Endlessly, it seemed, the blacks advanced. They fell before the French guns, but for every one that fell, another came on. They could no more have been turned back at that moment than could the great waves crashing against the rocks along the coast.

Rochambeau and his officers fled to an English ship in the harbor. It was finally over, the last battle France would ever fight on the soil of Saint Domingue. All that night and the two days that followed, the blacks raged through the city, burning, looting, killing the whites. Christophe and Dessalines made little effort to restrain them. They had suffered too long and too much. They would have to vent their fury before any order could be restored. The slaves had finally, in truth, become the masters. It was a new era and the country was from that time on to bear a new name, Haiti (the high place).

A new nation needed a new flag, and it is said that Dessalines created one with a single dramatic gesture. He seized the red, white and blue tricolor of France, tore out the strip of white and stamped it into the mud. When he had done that, he had himself declared governor general for life, with the right to name his successor. It was hardly an auspicious beginning for a nation struggling toward liberty and equality. How much better it would have been for the Haitians if they had been able to achieve a constitution similar to that created by the American revolutionists to the north. Instead, they were plunged almost at once into a dictatorial pattern from which they have never since been able to escape.

If it is true that power corrupts and absolute power corrupts absolutely, no more striking example of that maxim can be found than in the bloody history of Haiti. Hardly had Dessalines seized power than he wanted more. Being governor general for life was not enough. He demanded a kingdom, an empire. In October of 1804 Jean Jacques Dessalines—child of the jungle and former slave, still unable to read or write—had himself declared emperor.

It was a move that surprised no one, least of all Christophe, who had been reinstated as governor of Cap Français. Christophe could see the changes that were taking place in Dessalines. He had turned from a man of action, a superb soldier, into a bejeweled fop with a crown on his head. Administration bored him. When his secretaries brought him sheaves of state papers, he scattered them with a wave of his hand. Only one thing had not really changed in Dessalines: his blood lust and thirst for cruelty. In a fit of temper or boredom, he had ordered every last Frenchman on the island to be killed, and he spent much of his time personally executing those who had not escaped. But even that pastime grew wearying. The supply of Frenchmen waiting to die was growing thin. And so Dessalines, the tiger of the jungle, the invincible warrior, took up dancing. He imported ornate uniforms and surrounded himself with pretty girls as he stumbled through the delicate paces of the minuet.

Haiti had lost all respect for Dessalines and his dancing masters. Business had come to a standstill and the people were starving. It could not go on much longer.

Christophe said nothing, but went about disassociating himself and the region of the north more and more from Dessalines's follies. Over the years Christophe had learned the value of patience. Let Dessalines hang himself. Christophe's time would come.

Come it did, on a blazing midsummer day as Emperor Jacques I rode with his retinue toward Port-au-Prince. Dessalines was in a depressed mood. His empire was torn by revolt. Word had come shortly before that the rebels were marching on Port-au-Prince and that it was only a matter of hours before the city would be in their hands.

When the news came, the dancing masters and pretty girls had trembled before his rage, but Dessalines was too busy to bother with them. Demanding his horse and saber, he swept off his fancy wig and fur-trimmed robes. With a dozen officers galloping behind, he raced toward Port-au-Prince. In fact, he never reached it. At the Red Bridge, on the outskirts of the city, soldiers suddenly appeared.

Brusquely, the emperor ordered them to attention. They failed to obey. With a bellow, he rode toward them, expecting his officers to follow. Instead, they melted away into the brush, leaving him to face the ambush alone. Dessalines had never in his life retreated from anything. Cursing the rebels, he rode straight into their middle. Fifty rifles were pointed in his direction, but no one fired. The peasant soldiery had a superstitious awe of the great Dessalines, the Emperor. Could an ordinary bullet kill such a man?

As if to answer that question, a fourteen-year-old boy on the edge of the crowd suddenly raised his gun and fired—not at the emperor but at his horse. The beast crumpled and Dessalines went down. Reaching for his saber, he tried to get up. A bayonet point tore his cheek. It seemed to be what the mob was waiting for. Like vultures, they fell upon him, hacked him to bits, and left his mutilated body by the side of the road.

7

WITH THE DEATH of Dessalines, Christophe was next in line. But for what? To rule a bankrupt country torn by revolt and civil war? It was not a pleasing prospect. Still, Christophe could no more have backed away from the opportunity to rule than could Toussaint or Dessalines. Christophe knew he had much to learn from the death of Dessalines. In a way, their careers had been very similar. They had both been slaves and then soldiers, and both had come up through the ranks by force of bravery, personality and ambition. And where had that rise taken Dessalines? To brief glory and then to a bloody end on a dusty roadway near his capital city.

Dessalines had failed because he had been a soldier, not a ruler. When it came to killing, no one could do it better than Jean Jacques. But it was not killing that put bread in the mouths of the people and brought income from the plantations. Ruling did that—ruling that took into account the need for imports and exports, the investment of foreign capital, peace and commerce, all the details of everyday life that had bored Jean Jacques and made him howl with rage.

Christophe would do it differently. His people were waiting to see if he would accept the position of president of the new state of Haiti. First he wanted to see exactly what he would be president of. For a month he rode about the country, carrying a telescope, and from every hilltop he surveyed burned-out plantations, ruined refineries, fought-over villages, starving peasants.

The people were lazy now. They had won their freedom, and what was freedom for but to lounge and sleep and watch the babies playing in the dust? Why plow and cultivate and hack sugar cane? One could always live on plantains and an occasional scrap of meat. They had gotten rid of their hard-driving white masters. Would they accept another master now simply because he was black?

It would be Christophe's job to force them back into the pattern they had come to hate. They must work, rebuild, replant. As he gazed out across the countryside, he had a vision of the future. Foreign ships waiting in the harbor, bringing gold in return for the limitless produce grown in the rich soil of

Haiti. Wealth for all of them, and respect from the world's great powers. An independent black nation, rich and secure. His people had been driven to war, forced to fight against the foreign invaders. Now they must be driven to work with the same intensity. It was a program which Dessalines, in his short-sightedness, had been unable to conceive, but he, Christophe, could see it all and turn the dream to reality.

He returned to his city (which had been renamed Cap Haitien, to remove the last vestige of the hated French) and announced his decision. He would assume the presidency, but only on his own terms. His people needed a firm hand and masterful direction. He would give them both.

The people's reply was not quite what he wanted, but it was good enough. They made him generalissimo of Haiti's land and sea forces. He would take what power they gave him and in time (like those who had gone before him and those who would come after) he would seize more. The new nation was like a skittish horse; it needed gentling at first and then a firm hand. He, who had been a stableboy for so many years, understood the technique.

On February 17, 1807, Henri Christophe took command of the Haitian ship of state. That it was bankrupt and nearly sinking was clearly evident to the new captain, but he had no reservations about the course he would steer. What he wanted was a strong, prosperous Haiti with a powerful army. Why the army? First, because the new nation was already torn by civil war (in the south at Port-au-Prince a mulatto leader named Pétion had established a government of his own and was at war with Christophe's northern forces), and second (this was to become the overriding passion of his life), because he was convinced that some day the French would come back.

Christophe's first move was to send an army to the south to deal with Pétion. It was a mistake. To this day, historians are not quite sure what happened. Christophe's army swept all before it, right to the gates of Port-au-Prince. There something went wrong. Did Christophe grow weary of the chase and capriciously order his army home or did Pétion muster his troops for one last battle and manage to defeat the black giant of the north? The second premise seems more likely. In any case, Christophe never did capture Port-au-Prince. He called his army back to Cap Haitien. Pétion—a poet and intellectual rather than a man of war—was content to leave the situation that way: a country divided in half with two rulers.

To Pétion, Christophe was hardly more than a savage, another brutal black leader in the tradition of Dessalines. He would end, Pétion felt sure, the same way Dessalines had ended: hacked to death by his own people. What Pétion failed to take into account was Christophe's almost incredible energy and ambition and his surprising grasp of the basic facts of economy. Power, Christophe knew, came with prosperity. The treasury was empty and his first job would be to fill it. But how? The answer was unbelievably simple.

The fields of Haiti burgeon in the hot sun. Throw a seed on the ground and the green leaves wriggle forth almost overnight. Wild creepers bind the trees like snakes. Fruit can be had for the picking. One does not even need a bowl or dish for eating, for these too are supplied free by a bountiful nature. Gourd vines are everywhere and one has only to pluck a gourd and scrape it clean to have a perfectly fine bowl. The simple people of the thatched huts prefer the gourd to any other utensil.

Very well, then, reasoned Christophe (who himself dined off golden plates), if the gourds are what the peasants value, they must somehow be turned into cash. But how? Who will buy a gourd? Only the peasants themselves—and they will not buy them as long as they can pick them free. Furthermore, they have no money to buy them with. But they have something else. Coffee, for instance . . .

At once, Christopher ordered his soldiers out into the countryside to pick every gourd they could find. Christophe's men took them all—those privately owned and those which belonged to no one. The peasants offered no objection. How could they? He was Christophe the ruler, the strong man. The fact that he was black too did not make him any more merciful.

Within a week, the capital city was bulging with gourds. By the hundreds of thousands they were stacked under armed guard. When he had them all, Christophe sent word that gourdes could be purchased from the government: a gourd for a handful of coffee beans. The farmers began to pick coffee

beans and exchange them for gourds. As the piles of gourds shrank, they were replaced by hills of coffee beans. Christophe promptly sold the coffee to foreign traders. Instead of coffee, he was now accumulating gold. It was all so simple.

European merchants were arriving daily at Cap Haitien. They could do business with Christophe. A tyrant he might be, but he did not have Dessalines's pathological hatred of the whites or Pétion's dreamy impracticality.

Others came as well—professors to establish schools, ambassadors to represent their countries' interests. The world was beginning to respect the ignorant stableboy who still could not read or write. Christophe was a mover and a shaker. He could make things hum.

Far to the south, Pétion heard the news and pretended to be amused. So Christophe was making a great man of himself. He was building a palace and a fortress unlike any ever conceived of before by a black man. But that took money, and money could only be got from the labor of the people and the people would not work without being driven. If they were driven, it simply meant they had exchanged one form of slavery for another.

Just wait, said Pétion. Wait for the day when they will tear him to pieces.

8

IT IS NOT ONLY the lush tropical growth that springs so wildly from the soil of Haiti. Dreams grow there too—improbable fantasies of pomp and nobility, the panoply of kings. And why should not an ex-slave have as much right to the trappings of royalty as any other man?

Who can say at what point Christophe decided to make himself king? Perhaps it was not his idea at all. Perhaps it was Vastey's idea.

Pompée Valentin Vastey, son of a white father and a mulatto mother, was chief counselor to the magnificent Christophe. Officially his position was that of secretary, but he had gradually become an adviser on all matters of state. Very likely it was he who nourished Henri's ambitions.

Yet why not? If Napoleon, who had risen from a corporal, had the right to declare himself emperor, why should not Christophe, who had been a sergeant, call himself king? The people would respect him for it, and so would foreigners—even the French. As it was, with Haiti divided under rulers in both the north and the south, Bonaparte might contemplate another invasion. But if Haiti had a king, a king who built himself a great palace and dined off golden plates . . . why then . . . was not Christophe a natural king, perhaps the descendant of African rulers? At last he had come back to his birthright.

Christophe was a man in a hurry. He was forty years old, no longer the laughing young giant who had thumbed his nose at Leclerc's invading army. If they wanted him to be king, then king he would be. But he would need a kingdom first, and the proper buildings to go with it.

Building was something Christophe understood. After all, he had been sold as a slave to a stonemason. Whereas Dessalines had been content to while away his time with dancing lessons, he, Christophe, King Henri I, would be known as the Builder. The one who transformed dreams into mortar and stone. The one who would build himself memorials and monuments such as no black man—and few whites either—had ever conceived.

Leclerc had installed himself as governor general with pomp and ceremony. The coronation of King Henri would surpass that occasion by far.

Every stonemason, plasterer and carpenter had been ordered by royal decree to report to the king. When they were assembled, he took them to a pile of smoke-blackened ruins in the center of the town and told them what he wanted.

"A church once stood here," said the king, "an ordinary church. It was burned to the ground during the war. Indeed, I burned it myself. Now I want it rebuilt. But not as it was before. I want the biggest and most magnificent church this island has ever seen. And I want it ready for my coronation two months from today."

Two months later to the day, Henri I was crowned in the chapel of his new church. They put a crown on his head and a jeweled scepter in his hand and called him the first of a hereditary line of royalty. If he was to be king, he needed nobles, so with his customary energy Henri had created them. At his coronation he was surrounded by barons, dukes and princes, all former slaves, cane cutters, dish washers. The magnificence of their robes outshone anything worn at Versailles. The ceremony itself was unmatched in the history of the New World. That gigantic black man in his royal robes and jewels was a unique figure.

Henri was a man of flamboyant and regal tastes. Even as governor, he had lived in the most splendid house obtainable. Now, as king, he required a palace. With his customary urgency, he set about building one.

It was called Sans-Souci and he built it at Milot, some twenty miles from the sea. One may wonder at the choice of site until one remembers that Henri always had that obsession about the return of the French. He did not want his palace in Cap Haitien, where it could be quickly cut off by invading forces. Milot was then (and is little changed today) a sleepy country town of small huts and wandering goats. Only a Christophe could have thought of erecting a palace there. Or did he, even then, see in his mind's eye the mighty fortress that would some day rise above Milot?

He had built his cathedral in two months; in less than a year, with monies derived from his personal plantations, he completed his palace—all with native labor, masons, architects. The palace stood four stories above the highest terrace. There were banquet halls, grand stairways, private rooms for the king and queen, the prince royal and princesses;

stables, gardens, arsenals, a printing shop, quarters for the royal guard—it went on and on. The rooms were paved with marble, and a mountain stream had been diverted to run beneath the floors to keep them cool. The finest tapestries and paintings had been imported from Europe to cover the walls.

All this was accomplished in a year, and involved a fantastic amount of correspondence with art dealers, importers, shipping concerns. Vastey ran by Christophe's side like a small, faithful dog as the king directed the construction. It was said that Henri often dictated a hundred letters a day. Vastey got it all down on paper, and then the king, with stiff fingers that had been far more accustomed to the grip of a saber, would take the pen and laboriously scribble his name.

He would arrive from nowhere, storming down out of the hills on his white horse, and woe betide the luckless workman caught napping in the shade. Often the king himself, in a dusty uniform, would take up the mason's trowel to speed the work. Then he was off again, only to return sometimes at night —a tall, solitary figure striding the empty terrace, gazing about him at the half-finished walls. On occasion he was there all night so he could spur the workers on again at dawn.

And when it was done at last, he held court. The king and his queen (Marie-Louise, daughter of the

hotelkeeper who had been Henri's master when he was still a slave) sat on a raised dais. Below stood the nobles, courtiers, advisers and officers: the Count of Limonade and the Duke of Marmelade; a doctor from Edinburgh; a mathematician from London; a priest from Paris. The peasants, barefoot and humble, came to beg the king's pardon for their presence and to plead for his mercy.

The king drove himself to the limit and he expected no less of his subjects. Fits of anger now seized him like a fever; his rage was becoming legendary. He was worse, the people muttered, than the French had been. And he was everywhere—riding, thrashing, punishing, building. No duke, count, prince or baron was safe from his wrath. He had issued the Code Henri, under which every ablebodied man and woman in the kingdom was required to work. The hours of labor were irrevocably established: dawn to dusk, with breakfast on the spot and time off only for the two hottest hours of the day.

Nor were the nobles and landowners allowed to live in idle luxury. Henri was at least a hundred years ahead of his time in securing workmen's benefits and compensation. Hospital and medical care was to be furnished for every worker, at the cost of the landlord. No worker could be ejected from the owner's land on the grounds of illness or inability to work. When a man or woman grew too old to work, he must be retired and his employer must support him for life. There were no absentee landlords. Those who did not live on their land and exploit every last inch of it would lose it. A prince or baron could be demoted to peasant overnight if he did not make the most of his holdings. The Code Henri was as rigid in its social reforms as was the court etiquette which required every last button of every uniform to be in place.

Where was the lazy, tropical life of Saint Domingue? Gone forever, it seemed, under the lash of this imperious man.

9

WHY THE RELENTLESS haste? Why try to accomplish in a year or five or ten what no blacks had accomplished in thousands of years of recorded history? Henri had an answer to that too, one he gave to visiting diplomats and ambassadors.

"My people," he would say, "are as old as yours, or older. And there are as many black men in Africa as there are white men in Europe. Yet we have been turned into slaves, exploited, driven blindly like cattle. Only in Haiti have we competed with you on your own terms and defeated you. Why? Because at last we have a sense of pride. Until now the black man has had no sense of history, no pride. No monuments, no buildings to last beyond his lifetime or the lifetimes of his children. Here we will change all that. Here we will build and produce. Here, at last, we will have a sense of pride . . ."

Most Europeans came prepared to be amused by the glittering pretensions of Christophe and his court. Yet once they were there at Sans-Souci, in the actual presence of the king, they knew that whatever else he might be, King Henri I was certainly no joke.

As the land prospered, so did the king. Indeed, he *was* the land, or the principal holder of most of it. From his palace window he could look out upon mile after mile of cane fields shivering in the wind, all of it the personal property of the king. And when he tired of that view, he could move to another palace, for he had built seven more, only slightly smaller than Sans-Souci. From each he enjoyed the same vista, mile after mile of the king's cane and cattle and coffee, all waiting to be harvested and turned into foreign gold. In one year his plantations had accounted for two-thirds of the kingdom's exports. The once bankrupt island now enjoyed the most stable currency in the West Indies. Indeed, he had so much gold that it was becoming a problem to know what to do with it. He began to think of a place where it could all be put, where it could be protected forever.

He began to look speculatively at the mountains around him and at one in particular—a jagged peak which seemed to rear straight up into the sky and which was known as the Bonnet.

A fortress in the sky, a citadel atop an unscalable peak, a fortress to withstand the onslaught of any army. To Pétion in the south it seemed the final absurdity of Christophe's regime. Pétion was convinced that the French would never return, and even if they did, they would surround Christophe's mountain and starve him out. If the French could not get in, it would be equally true that Christophe could not get out.

Most of Haiti agreed. The Leclerc expedition had been a costly disaster. Surely the mighty Bonaparte, acclaimed as the world's best general, could not be such a fool as to try it again.

They were partly right. Bonaparte would never try it again. He was, in fact, already heading toward his own decline and fall. He would be defeated and exiled, and return, to be defeated once more, and finally exiled to a lonely speck of land in the South Atlantic. There he would meet his death.

What Christophe realized and what Pétion seemed to have forgotten was that the rich ex-colonists of Saint Domingue had never given up the hope of some day recovering their lands. No sooner had Louis XVIII ascended the throne of France than they were at it again. A petition was presented to the French Chamber of Deputies requesting an investigation of conditions in Haiti. Incredible as it now seems, the commission returned a report saying that in their opinion the blacks of Haiti would welcome a return to the sovereignty of France. It was recommended that such an offer be made to the blacks and that, if their answer was in the negative, sufficient land and sea forces be sent to take the island.

How could any member of the French government have supposed that either Christophe or Pétion would welcome a return to French rule? The French politicians showed abysmal ignorance as well as arrogance in imagining that the Haitians, who had shed so much blood and fought so hard for independence, would now give it up at a snap of the French king's fingers.

Christophe's answer was immediate and couched in his usual dignified terms. He replied that the King of Haiti would deal with the King of France only as one independent power to another and that all such communications should be passed through the usual diplomatic channels.

Pétion, in Port-au-Prince, replied that at the first appearance of a hostile force he would set fire to all the buildings in the city and destroy everything that could not be removed to the mountains.

Neither leader, black Henri or mulatto Pétion, had

failed to observe the last line of the French commission's report, which had urged the immediate dispatch of an expedition to put the ex-colonists in possession of their former estates and to establish laws for the regulation of the colony, "with a view to the blacks who were already there and THOSE WHO SHOULD HEREAFTER BE INTRODUCED."

Clearly, the horrible specter of slavery was far from dead.

Meanwhile, the difference between the two regimes—Christophe's in the north and Pétion's in the south—grew ever more striking. It was the difference between a dictatorial government under the rule of an obsessed king and an easygoing republic where each man did pretty much as he pleased and worked only when the spirit or necessity moved him. Christophe was hated by much of the peasantry but respected by all. Pétion was beloved by all but respected by few. The very qualities which endeared him to his people made him unfit to control them. Moreover, he was a mulatto, part of a minority group in a land populated largely by blacks.

The spark of liberty in the New World which had been ignited in the United States and fanned to a flame in Haiti was spreading to other areas as well. Simón Bolívar was leading the struggle for independence in South America. He had few friends, but among them was Pétion. Pétion had secretly equipped Bolívar with rifles, powder, cartridges and all kinds of provisions. It was a dangerous move for Pétion, since it might well have produced a Spanish invasion of Port-au-Prince, but he was moved to it by his sincere desire to assist in freeing the slaves of South America. After liberating Venezuela, Bolívar sent Pétion a golden sword inscribed, "To the author of our liberties."

Pétion was a kindly man, a poet, cultured, well-read. Like many others of that type, he was ahead of his time. Since the mulattoes were a minority group, he felt it necessary to lean over backwards in his efforts to conciliate the blacks. He was certainly intelligent enough to realize, as had Christophe, that agriculture was the only source of Haiti's revenue and that it must be increased, but he did not dare to drive the people to work, nor was he in a position to punish idleness or crime. Above all, he did not see himself as another Dessalines.

Dessalines is Haiti's hero. A statue bearing his name stands in Port-au-Prince. It is a curious likeness, having the face of a thin-lipped, straight-nosed aristocrat. He wears a cocked hat and brandishes a sword, but his stony eyes convey nothing of the passion and blood lust that are associated with his name. The visitor to Port-au-Prince may well find it difficult to associate the statue with the man, and for good reason. The one has nothing to do with the other. The statue is not of Dessalines at all but was ordered by some unknown Central American president who was cast out of office or assassinated before the statue was delivered. Since the Haitians were getting ready to order a statue of their national hero anyway, they decided to buy this one cheap. No one seemed to be bothered by the fact that, except for the sword and the hat, it did not resemble Dessalines in any way.

Nor does the heroic legend of him as the national benefactor fit any better. True, he drove the whites out—but Dessalines liked to fight and kill. When he was a French general under Leclerc, he slaughtered blacks with the same avidity he had displayed toward whites. It was Dessalines who ordered that a hundred blacks be killed for having assaulted one white officer, and who, when he became emperor, slaughtered every white man he could find and left the naked bodies lying in the streets until they rotted. When it took too long to dig the whites out of their hiding places, he announced a general amnesty, offering safety to all who would swear allegiance to him. One by one, the terrified whites crept from their lairs. When he had them all assembled in the public square, Dessalines ordered his troops to open fire.

Dessalines was a butcher. That Rochambeau, the French commander after Leclerc, was an equally avid butcher hardly lessens the weight of Dessalines's crimes.

To Pétion, all this was self-evident. He wanted to rule in peace and brotherhood—but what brotherhood could there be between white and brown and black? Sometimes he hated and feared the blacks, and at other times he loved them. Unlike the whites and mulattoes, the blacks laughed easily. Pétion, the poet, made them laugh and they loved him for it. But to be loved in a bankrupt country beset by enemies was not enough.

Far to the north, King Henri was going ahead with his mad scheme of building a fortress in the sky. No one loved him for it, but that was immaterial to Henri. Stone and brick and mortar and gunpowder and gold were the stuff of power, not love.

10

THE KINGDOM PROSPERED, but the king was not content. Time was his enemy. There was so much to do and so little time. There were schools, roads, palaces, fortifications, ships and docks to be built. He was determined to yank his people from the sleepy life of the jungle straight into the hustle of Western civilization. Above all, he was determined that the children be taught to read and write, though the sovereign himself could barely sign his own name.

Henri was far from uninformed. He spent the daylight hours spurring the people on to work, but in the evenings, while the soft dusk settled over Sans-Souci, he called Vastey or his Scottish doctor or one of his other foreign advisers in to read to him. Journals were brought from England and France and through them the king was kept informed on world affairs, trade, education, architecture, whatever was his passion of the moment.

It was in one such journal that he learned of the teaching methods of the Lancaster Foreign School Society of London. Henri at once engaged in correspondence with the society and brought six teachers to Haiti. He asked them to describe their school buildings in London, and almost overnight, replicas of the British schools were built in a dozen different areas of the kingdom. The six Englishmen were of course not enough to staff the schools, but educated blacks and mulattoes were found and put through a rapid course of instruction. Within a matter of weeks, the schools were in operation and two thousand children were being taught to write not only in their native Creole but in English and Spanish as well. Henri dreamed of the day when he would either buy the Spanish part of the island or take it by force. He wanted one island, one black kingdom, and he did not want language to be a barrier.

In addition, he founded a royal college for advanced students and arranged for his own Scottish physician to lecture there on anatomy and surgery. To the educated Pétion, in Port-au-Prince, all this must have come as strange news indeed. He had regarded Christophe as little more than a despotic barbarian;

yet here was the black ruler beating him at his own game.

Christophe was even more ambitious when it came to the education of his own children. The two princesses, Améthyste and Athénaire, must be taught all the manners and graces that befitted their royal station. For this purpose, two maiden ladies were imported from Philadelphia, at that time reputed to be the American seat of culture and propriety. History has not recorded their names and we can only imagine their astonishment when they disembarked under the blazing Haitian sun and were escorted to the palace of Sans-Souci—a more splendid structure than anything they had ever seen in Philadelphia. Imagine too their reaction to the gigantic black king and his court of nobles dressed in white and scarlet. Footmen, pages, royal guards—all of it more opulent than they could have conceived and all of it set in the sleepy little village of Milot, with the mountains looming close by and the jungle thrusting in at the doors.

The children were well mannered and the queen was most pleasant, but the king—well, the king was another matter. He was a whirlwind of activity. If he slept at all, it could not have been for more than four or five hours a night, and he seemed to expect his court to maintain the same pace. Courtiers who gathered in the palace hallways to whisper together would scatter like chickens at the approach of a hawk when the king strode through. And always he had with him that long brass telescope, so that hardly anyone was safe from his spying. There were ugly rumors of the punishment for idleness. It was said that he had once looked through his telescope, had seen a peasant asleep under a tree and had gone into such a rage that he had trained a cannon on the man with his own hands and blown him to bits. The ladies might have found that a little hard to believe, but it was certainly not hard to believe the king's mania to build his fortress, his citadel in the sky.

The project had begun with Dessalines, but he had lacked King Henri's drive and organization, and so it had remained little more than a dream. For the first seven years of his reign Henri too had been busy with other matters. If he was inclined from time to time to forget the citadel, Vastey was always there to remind him. Of them all, Vastey had the greatest phobia about the return of the French.

It is doubtful if even then Henri regarded the project in precisely Vastey's terms. He had been a general for too many years, had fought against too many enemies, had conducted too many raids and retreats to be beguiled by the concept of a static defense. It was true that an impregnable fortress could be built atop the Bonnet, but it was equally true that if an enemy held all the ground below, the fortress must some day fall. If the French were to return, Christophe would have to fight them again as he had fought in the past, making the jungle and the impassable mountains his allies, using fire and destruction and fever as his weapons.

What, then, was it that the king really saw in his citadel? An eternal monument, more than likely, a project to rival those of the Pharaohs, a structure with which his name and the ambitions and skills of black men would be forever linked. What the king wanted was a fist in the sky for all the world to see. It would be visible twenty miles at sea, the most impressive structure of the New World, a monument to black pride and ambition.

The king had magnified Dessalines's concept many times and now it was brought to final form with the aid of a Haitian engineer named Henri Besse. It was to be an immense stone battleship in the sky, with its prow pointing magnetic north and its decks ringed with 365 great bronze cannon, one for each day of the year. The walls of the stone ship were to be 130 feet high and 30 feet thick—and all built on the spiny tip of a mountain up which the nimblest donkey could barely scramble.

If the citadel were ever besieged, it had to be self-sufficient. There must be hundreds of casks of gunpowder and hundreds of thousands of fifty-pound cannon balls. There would be a gigantic underground

cistern to catch every drop of rain that fell on the mountain. There must be dungeons, treasure troves and store rooms to supply enough food for ten thousand men. There must be a parade ground, a palace for the king and quarters for his nobles and their families.

The nobles shook their heads when they heard of King Henri's dream. Impossible, they thought. The king only snorted. They had thought every one of his projects impossible. Nothing was impossible to a man who had fire and ambition and wealth. He, the king, had enough of all three to accomplish anything he wanted, and what he wanted now above all else was his citadel. It was to be his everlasting monument. What he could not have foreseen was that it was also to be his tomb.

11

ALL DAY in the blazing sun the line of men crawled up and down the mountain like ants—exhausted, sweating, staggering under their burdens. Every twenty feet along the line of march stood one of the king's soldiers, armed with gun and whip. Let one of the bearers stumble or pause for breath and the lash would reach out to draw blood. The naked, sweating men, thousands of men, came and went. There were criminals among them and simple peasants and those who had plotted treason against the king. They came from every strata of society up to and including noblemen who had aroused the king's displeasure. The king, in his frenzy, spared no one.

At first, the task seemed hopeless. The mountain was too steep, the climate too exhausting, the loads too heavy. Men engaged in such an incredible undertaking would die by the thousands. Even if they were replaced by others, more would die. It seemed the king had gone mad and in his madness would destroy them all.

Henri himself often stripped off his uniform tunic to help lift one of the great stone blocks into place. It was hardly the kind of action one might expect from a king, and particularly from one so conscious of his majesty as Henri. Yet it was not too surprising when one remembers that this king had once been a slave boy. If he demanded too much of his people, he demanded even more of himself. His workers watched in superstitious awe as the king heaved blocks of stone which would have broken the back of an ordinary man.

There were times when the king could be seen working alone by torchlight far into the night. At such times he would allow no one else to accompany him to the work on the walls, and it was rumored that he was secretly burying vast hoards of gold. To this day the rumors persist and treasure hunters pick the bones of Henri's citadel in a vain search for his hidden gold. If he did indeed bury his treasure there, he did it well enough to resist a century of searching.

All state business became secondary to the assault on the mountain. No one was safe from the king's rage. Duke Richard, governor of the Cap and the second most powerful man in the kingdom, was put to work on the walls like a common criminal because he had incurred the king's displeasure. Poets, statesmen and archbishops were sent to join him. When they fell from the mountain or died of exhaustion, the king only shrugged. People had become meaningless to him; it was only the unyielding stone that mattered.

Pride, the king told his people, mattered more than life. The stone would outlive them all. The fortress would be a monument for all time to their pride and dignity. The mountain must be defeated at whatever cost.

It was said that twenty thousand men died in the building of the citadel. Very likely each block of stone that went into those massive walls cost a man's life. Only a tyrant could have recruited so many workers and driven them up the mountain. The citadel was being built; the king was indeed defeating the mountain, but at what a cost! There was no joy in the kingdom. No one dared laugh. When a witty courtier made a little joke about the native coffee beans, he was dispatched at once to the walls. As the king's severity increased, his people grew more restless.

Even Vastey was afraid of him now. When he tried to reason with Henri, the king either ignored him or listened in sullen silence as Vastey pointed out that the people were growing rebellious under the intolerable burdens imposed on them.

Corneille Brelle, the French priest, had been the king's religious adviser for many years. It was Brelle who had officiated at Henri's coronation and who had seen to the religious education of the crown prince and the princesses. Now word was brought to the king that Brelle too was guilty of treason. He had been in correspondence with the king's enemy, Pétion. Letters had been found concealed in his chambers. Henri ordered Brelle beheaded, and not even the intervention of the British ambassador could save him.

12

HENRI COULD BUY or bludgeon all but time. Though he was only fifty, he thought of himself as an old man. There was much to do and so little time. He had been so obsessed with the citadel that he had given little thought to anything else. Now he began to think once again of his family. What would happen to them when he was gone? Without his power and strength, the queen would never be able to hold his rebellious subjects in line. He must provide for her. He put aside six million dollars in gold coins and had it shipped off to England, to be held there in her name. An equal quantity of gold was left with trusted advisers who would turn it over to Marie-Louise after his death.

Death, he was convinced, would be coming for him soon. He brooded about it at night when, unable to sleep, he stood alone on the battlements of the citadel, surrounded by the bronze snouts of his cannon gleaming coldly in the moonlight. From that vantage point, he could look down into the valleys and across to the other peaks. The great dark island spread out before him, its blackness punctuated only by the light of an occasional cooking fire. Down there were some who loved him and many more who hated him. That no longer mattered. All he cared about was that they should feel a sense of pride in what he had accomplished, for he had not been building a private monument for himself but one in their name. It was almost finished now, the great citadel that would outlast them all.

Henri Christophe was growing old and tired. During all the years of campaigning against the French, he had slept on the ground in heat and cold and never felt it, but now he found that the night wind nipped at his flesh, cleaving to the bone. When sleep eluded him, as it so often did, he would amuse himself by playing a solitary game of billiards. Once a billiard marker at the little hotel by the waterfront, the king loved the game. And one of the first things he had installed in the citadel was a billiard table.

Perhaps it was after just such a sleepless night that Henri Christophe set off in midday heat on his last mad ride along the dusty road to Limonade. Hens, goats and sleepy-eyed peasants scattered at his approach. Anxious mothers seized their naked

children and hid them inside the huts as they heard the thunder of hoofs. When he was gone, with the dust boiling up behind him, they shook their heads. Had it indeed been the king who had pounded by on his white horse, or some voodoo spirit of the woods?

He reined his lathered horse up before the chapel at Limonade and slid from the saddle. His legs almost buckled under him, but when one of the villagers dared to offer a helping hand, the king thrust it away. His horse stood with hanging head, sides heaving. Ordinarily, Henri would have concerned himself first with the welfare of the animal, but now he did not give it even a backward glance as he entered the chapel.

Why had the king elected to visit the Church of Saint Anne that day at that particular time? No one knew. Nor did anyone dare ask. Even the plump Breton priest, dozing in his hammock, was struck with fear when informed that the king was at prayer in his church.

Hurriedly, the priest donned his robes and made his way toward the chapel, where the king was kneeling before the altar, his broad shoulders almost filling the narrow room. Then, to the priest's horror, the king let out a muffled groan and clutched at the wooden altar to support himself. His weight was too great and the altar crashed to the floor. Henri swayed and then collapsed, face down on the stone floor.

The priest scurried for help. At first the villagers hid from him. The idea of laying hands on their king was beyond their comprehension. But at last half a dozen of them agreed to help and between them they managed to carry Henri's limp form to a bed in the priest's house. Then the bravest among them mounted the king's horse and galloped back to Sans-Souci to spread the word.

Within the hour the queen, the king's doctor and his personal bodyguard were at his side. They filled the tiny house until the doctor ordered all but the queen to wait outside.

The king had not moved. He lay rigid on the bed, his face and uniform smeared with blood. Only the slow rise and fall of his chest indicated life.

Outside the house, Vastey was issuing orders to the troops. A veil of absolute quiet and secrecy must surround the village of Limonade. He did not want so much as the crowing of a rooster or the bark of a dog to disturb the fallen monarch. Every animal for three miles must be removed immediately. And the roads must be sealed, no one to go in or out.

The villagers must be confined to their huts. On pain of death, no one was to approach the church.

Even Vastey did not dare enter the priest's house. Finally, Dr. Stewart, his thin Scottish face expressing extreme concern, emerged.

"Will he live?" said Vastey.

"He will live," Stewart answered, "but I doubt if he will recover. He has suffered a massive stroke and possible brain damage from the fall. Very likely he will be permanently paralyzed."

For two days the soundless village drowsed in the summer heat. Only Vastey, the doctor and the queen were allowed to enter the king's chamber. Henri had not moved. His features still bore the same gray pallor and his great fists remained clenched at his sides. But on the third day his eyelids fluttered open and he looked up into the eyes of Marie-Louise, who in all that time had hardly stirred from his side.

They carried him back to Sans-Souci on a litter. There was no way to keep the secret now and the word ran like a brush fire across the hills. The drums pounded out the message and the wind carried the sound of the drums.

"The King has fallen! Henri is dying!"

A great silence settled on the land. The villagers waited fearfully for the thunder of hoofs and the appearance of soldiers. Even the king's enemies dared not make a move. Henri was not yet dead, and while he lived, even though partially paralyzed, he retained the power.

Within weeks, all Henri's carefully structured kingdom began to fall apart. The peasants, tired of work, were resting on their hoes. The sugar cane rotted in the fields. Mulatto noblemen who had formerly danced attendance on the king were now absent from the palace. At last came the worst news of all—the garrison at Saint Marc had entered into negotiations with Pétion. Open revolt could not be far off.

Henri refused to remain in bed. Each day, four of his strongest soldiers carried him to the main hall of the palace or out onto the balcony. Sitting there with his telescope, he was able to look out over the green fields of his kingdom or up to the stone prow of the citadel. Although his legs were useless, his mind was as active as ever, and he was constantly devising ways of trying to hold his kingdom together.

News of the revolt at Saint Marc enraged him and he ordered that the ringleaders be brought to him at once in chains. He would personally have the pleasure of trying and condemning them. They would see that although the king could not walk, he was as powerful and cruel and quick to punish as ever.

But the general he had dispatched to put down the revolt never reached Saint Marc; he was shot and killed only a few miles from the palace. The rebels—their numbers swollen by others they had picked up along the way—had anticipated his move and were already marching on the palace. They were offering free rum and no work as inducements to the peasants. All along the dusty roads could be heard cries of *"A bas le Roi!* Down with the King!"

Henri reacted to the emergency with his characteristic energy. He could not afford to have traitors at his back as well as in front of him. Duke Richard of Marmelade had never forgiven Henri for the humiliation of being put to work as a common laborer on the walls of the citadel. Anticipating that Richard would lose no opportunity for revenge, the king ordered him to take the garrison from Cap Haitien (now Cap Henri) and march against the rebels.

Vastey was appalled when he heard the order and reminded the king that Richard would surely betray him.

Henri smiled. "Of course. But it is one of the oldest rules of warfare, Vastey, to concentrate all the enemy's forces in one position. He will take the garrison straight to Saint Marc to join the rebels. Then at least I will have them all in front of me."

Caught up in the king's enthusiasm, Vastey was almost able to forget for a moment that the king was paralyzed, the army in revolt and the kingdom literally crumbling. Henri had performed miracles before, and now, in his most desperate hour, he would somehow perform another.

As if to confirm this, Henri ordered a review of all his troops.

The next morning the king had his aides dress him in his most magnificent uniform—a combination of white silk and sky-blue satin—and then his bodyguards carried him outside and set him up on a throne-like chair on the great west terrace. Below, in the valley of Milot, the regiments were already assembled, five thousand crack troops of the army of Haiti. At the sight of the king they burst into spontaneous cheers. Henri waited until the roaring had subsided. Then he bellowed in a voice which could be heard by every one of the five thousand, "My horse!"

The king's white horse, already saddled, was waiting at the side of the terrace. At once a groom led it forward, its hoofs clicking on the stone floor. The king sat motionless until the horse was directly before him. As all eyes were riveted on him, he fought the single greatest battle of his life. To shouts of *"Vive le Roi!* Long live the King!" he began to push himself forward and upward, gripping the horse's mane with one hand and the saddle with the other. He prepared himself for the final effort to leap into the saddle as he had done so many thousands of times in the past, but suddenly his legs collapsed under him. With a groan, he released his hold on the saddle and slid down, so that he lay spread-eagled beneath the horse's belly.

The cheering died. The waves of sound, which had rolled from one rocky wall to the other, echoed one last time and were still. The queen and Vastey rushed forward and bent over the king. The bodyguards were summoned and lifted the king back into his chair.

They wanted to carry Henri back to his bed, but he ordered them all away, even the queen. Then he sat in the burning sun while the parade passed before him. As the regimental colors came into view, he held his right hand in a rigid salute. The men still cheered him, but the cheering had a hollow sound; it was as if from the moment they had seen their king lying helpless the soldiers had abandoned him. Indeed, as soon as they were out of sight, beyond the wall of the palace, their cheers turned to jeers. They joked among themselves about a king who

could not even mount his horse, and there were shouts of "*A bas le Roi! A bas Christophe!*"

The king held his salute until the last soldier had vanished. Then, to his surprise, he found himself almost alone. The nobles had gone. Even the servants had melted away in the wake of the troops. For the first time since its completion the palace of Sans-Souci was virtually deserted. Only the queen and the children, Vastey and Dr. Stewart and a few other faithful retainers were left. Now there was too much to do and too little time. The rebel army might arrive at any moment.

He knew that he could neither defend the palace nor get away to the citadel. Surely his own family could not drag his great weight up the mountain path—and who else was there to help? In any case, there was hardly time.

Drawing himself up in his chair, with something of the old tone of command in his voice, the king ordered the queen and Vastey to accompany the three children at once to Cap Henri, where they would take shelter in the English consulate. Vastey was to turn over to the queen the papers which showed her to be the rightful owner of the six million dollars in gold he had deposited in her name in England. Marie-Louise remained silent. She had no intention of complying with her husband's last command.

13

HE HAD SENT THEM all away and there was little to do now but wait. He lay on his bed in the great chamber which overlooked the valley, the old brass telescope still at his side.

Along the road that emerged from the forest they would come. There would be thousands of them, laughing, shouting, making a holiday out of the killing of an old, sick king. And afterward would they butcher him as they had Dessalines?

It no longer mattered what they did to him. It was finished now, all the dreams of pomp and glory. And when he was gone they would revert again to savagery. They would destroy his palace and raze his sugar refineries. They would go back to being lazy, illiterate peasants scratching a meager living from the land. He had tried to do too much with them, and there had never been enough time. In the end he had failed, as all men failed . . . But what a chase he had led them in his too brief reign! And as long as that great stone fortress rose into the sky above them, they would remember his name. *Christophe le Roi!* Christophe the King! *Christophe l'homme!* Christophe the man!

So they thought to have the fun of killing him, did they? Well, he had a surprise in store for them on that score too.

Orange blossoms of flame were appearing now. They were burning his houses, his mills, his cane, not even stopping to think they might use those things for themselves.

As they came closer to the palace, Christophe reached for the pistol which lay at his side. He loaded the charge and the golden bullet. He had always been extraordinarily fond of gold. It seemed only right for the king. As the first of them burst through the doorway, Christophe raised the pistol to his head and fired.

The mutilation he had expected never took place. Faithful Vastey and Marie-Louise saw to that. The queen's own jewelry and whatever gold Vastey could lay his hands on were used to bribe the looters. A king's ransom was strewn before the startled eyes of the mob. While they fought over it, Marie-Louise, the two princesses and Vastey removed the king's body from his bedchamber and placed it on a litter.

Slowly and carefully the few loyal ones started up the path to the mountain. The king was going back for the last time to the place he had loved best of all—the citadel.

As they neared the summit, they were seen by one of the sentries on the wall. A cry went up and in a moment hundreds of men were peering down at them.

A great shout was heard. "*Le Roi est mort!* The King is dead!"

For these men on the mountain, who had been unaware of what was happening down below, it was as if a trigger had been pressed. They burst out of the fortress by the hundreds—officers, soldiers, laborers, prisoners—rushing down to the valley to join the rebels. In an instant the citadel was as empty as Sans-Souci had been after the king had fallen before his army.

Only half a dozen loyal officers remained in the fortress. They came quickly down the slope to lend a hand with the body. What had to be done must be done within minutes, and then the queen and her children must be rushed to safety.

In the center of the courtyard was a great pit of builder's lime, newly mixed in preparation for the day's work. Wisps of smoke from the corrosive substance rose into the still air. Vastey nodded to one of the officers and together they lifted the heavy litter and carried it up the last few steps to the galley above the pit.

Around them were the 365 bronze cannon that had never been fired; below were the great walls that had never known an attacker. Marie-Louise and the girls stood at attention. Miles below in the valley the tiny figures of looters could be seen rushing in and out of the burning palace, but up here on the mountain no sound reached them but the sighing of the wind.

Vastey turned back the sheet to look for the last time at the face of his dead king. Then he picked up his end of the litter and with a great heave thrust the king's body down into the smoking lime.

Marie-Louise and the princesses escaped to Italy. They remained there for the rest of their lives and are buried in a tiny cemetery on the outskirts of Pisa. The crown prince was not so fortunate; he was murdered by the revolutionists.

Tourists visiting Haiti today can travel by car from the little port city of Cap Haitien to the village of Milot. There they can gaze in awe at the tumbled ruins of the palace of Sans-Souci. The more adventurous can hire burros to transport them up the trail to the citadel. Hour after hour, the trail winds up through the green forest. Native huts, much the same as those that stood there in Christophe's day, dot the way. To the casual visitor it seems hard to believe that almost every foot of that peaceful trail was once darkened with blood.

As you emerge from the somber green of the jungle onto the sun-swept rocks, the citadel rises before you. No visitor seeing it for the first time can help but feel a quickening of his pulse as he gazes up at the great stone edifice.

You enter by a small stone doorway, the same one through which the body of the king was dragged. The courtyard which contained the lime pit is rank with weeds. The bronze cannon, fallen from their mounts, still point down the mountain toward the enemy which never came. There is no sound but the sighing of the wind.

Index

Alligator Wood, 14, 16
Artibonite Valley, 35

Bastille, the, 12
Besse, Henri, 81
Bolívar, Simón, 74
Bonaparte, Napoleon, 21,
　22–5, 29, 32–3, 39, 41,
　42, 44, 45, 46, 61–2, 71
Bonnet, 71, 80
Brelle, Corneille, 87
Brunet, 40–1

Cap Français, 7–9, 12, 14, 16,
　21, 26–30, 34, 39, 42, 44,
　45, 47, 49; *see also* Cap
　Haitien and Cap Henri
Cap Haitien, 55, 57, 59, 64,
　85, 103; *see also* Cap
　Français and Cap Henri
Cap Henri, 95, 98; *see also*
　Cap Français and Cap
　Haitien

Christophe, Améthyste, 79,
　98, 101, 102, 103
Christophe, Athénaire, 79, 98,
　101, 102, 103
Christophe, Henri: childhood,
　5–6; arrives in Saint
　Domingue, 7; slave to
　naval officer, 9–10; slave
　to Negro, 11–17; in slave
　rebellion, 16; rise in black
　army, 20–1; commanding
　general, 25–48; governor
　of Cap Français, 49–55;
　inauguration as presi-
　dent, 55; coronation, 63;
　collapse, 91–2; death,
　101; burial, 102–3
Christophe, Marie-Louise,
　65–7, 88, 92, 93, 98, 101,
　102, 103
Church of Saint Anne, 91–2
citadel, 70–1, 76, 80–3, 84–6,
　88–9, 102–3, 104

Code Henri, 67–8

Dessalines, Jean Jacques, 33, 34–5, 40, 43, 47–51, 53, 57, 59, 62, 74–6, 80, 81, 100

flag, Haitian, 48
Franklin, Benjamin, 9
French presence: colonial slave rebellion, 13–17; invasion by French, 22–37; occupation by French, 39–48; resistance to French, 33–7, 42–3, 44–8; expulsion of French, 48
French Revolution, 12, 13

Gonaïves, 40
Grenada, 5

Honduras, 21

Jamaica, 18

Lancaster Foreign School Society of London, 78
LeBrun, 26–30
Leclerc, Charles, 23–30, 34, 35, 36, 40, 41, 42–3, 44–6, 47, 62, 63, 71, 75, 76
Leclerc, Pauline Bonaparte, 23–4, 31, 46
Limonade, 89, 91–3

Limonade, Count of, 67
Louis XVIII, 71, 72
Louverture, Toussaint, 15–16, 18–21, 22, 25, 26–7, 28, 29, 30, 33, 34, 35, 36, 40–1, 53

Marmelade, Duke Richard of, 67, 85–6, 95
Milot, 64, 79, 96, 103

Paris, 9, 14, 20, 21, 22, 23, 24
Pétion, 56–7, 59, 60, 71, 72–3, 74–6, 78, 87, 94
Port-au-Prince, 18, 34–5, 50–1, 56–7, 72, 74, 75, 78
Port-de-Paix, 19

Red Bridge, 50–1
Rochambeau, Donatien, Comte de, 46–7, 48, 76

Saint Kitts, 5
Saint Marc, 94, 95, 96
Sans Souci, 64–7, 70, 77, 79, 92, 93–8, 99, 102, 103
schools, 78–9
Stewart, Dr., 67, 77, 78, 92–3, 98

Vastey, Pompée Valentin, 61, 65, 77, 80, 86, 92, 93, 95, 96, 97, 98, 101, 102, 103

yellow-fever epidemic, 42–7